Let's Share A Story

Let's Share A Story

Stories from round the world to read aloud

Introduction by Jennie Ingham

Blackie

British Library Cataloguing in Publication Data
Let's share a story.
  823′.01′089282[J]   PZ7

ISBN 0-216-92076-0

Blackie and Son Ltd
7 Leicester Place
London WC2H 7BP

Printed in Great Britain by
Thomson Litho Ltd, East Kilbride, Scotland

Contents

Introduction

Most parents, being mere mortals, have willingly succumbed to the obvious charms of piped and bottled stories, on tape and television – and why not? Many a child has become an avid reader after seeing a story brought to life on 'Jackanory', or hearing it told on tape by a well-known actor. The paths to 'reading readiness' are many, varied, and often surprising.

Yet, for a small child, surely, nothing can replace the totally delightful experience of sharing a story with a caring, interested, involved adult.

Even now, I can remember the comfortable feeling of curling up on Grandad's knee in the dilapidated armchair; I can see the 'Prince Albert' moustache, the twinkling eyes and the wrinkles around them; smell the pipe tobacco and the pages of the book; feel the shiny illustrated paper, and visualize the pictures of fairies, monsters, mythical kings and queens, and enchanted woods. The story itself was but a part of this total experience. Furthermore, there was no sense of duty, educational purpose, or grinding chore – just pure unalloyed pleasure, for adult as well as child.

In any case, folktales have never been the sole province of children. Worldwide, they have been part of ritual, ceremony and religion; they have been told by midwives to distract women in labour from the pangs of childbirth; they have been used by prophets and in sagas to explain religious doctrine and moral values; they have been told by villagers spinning cotton to relieve the boredom and monotony; they have been told by fearful and incredulous humanity to explain the movements of the planets and the shapes of the earth – and to help us organize, objectify and cope with the emotions and ideas which are common to us all.

Yet there *are* differences between folktales and fairy tales of different countries, even between different versions of the same tale. Joseph Jacobs, the famous folklorist, wrote: 'Soils and national characters differ; but fairy tales are the same in plot and incident, if not in treatment'.

A fine example, included in this anthology, of different treatment of a story which will be familiar to most readers, ancient and modern, is *The Enchanted*

Palace, a haunting, dreamy Indian version of the *Sleeping Beauty* story, told here from the point of view of the Prince.

Readers will doubtless be familiar, too, with the story of *The Hare and the Tortoise*, which embodies the common theme of the slow and steady animal who wins the race. The version included in this collection differs from that which, no doubt, like me, you know from Aesop's Fables, in that it has been told by a Greek father who has settled in this country. His grandmother told him the story, which now he tells to his children. You will find that carrots have a vital role to play in his retelling!

And 'telling' is important, for the other vital aspect of sharing a story is the human voice. Storytelling is an essential part of our lives whether we are telling a fairy tale, reminiscing, or recounting yesterday's incident to a friend or neighbour. The human voice, the facial expression, the gesture all go together to bring the story to life. Before the child can internalize all this, the adult needs to breathe life into the print.

This collection, too, will give ample choice and variety for every palate and mood. The stories have been chosen to represent as many cultures as possible. This is especially important, as we have recently experienced a revival of the folklore and of storytelling in this country, encouraged by the many ethnic minority groups who have enriched our culture immeasurably by sharing with us their own storytelling traditions.

All the stories in this collection can be read aloud in about ten minutes by parents and teachers, and can be easily understood by young children. As you read, you cannot help but hear and feel the difference in mood and style, between the measured, rhythmic tones of *Koi-Ai and her Lost Shoe* from China and the cocky, cheeky style of the Anansi stories from the Caribbean.

You will find old favourites like *The Three Billy Goats Gruff*, or *Hansel and Gretel*, alongside intriguing new titles like *The Willow-Leaf Eyebrow*, also from China.

The full colour illustrations have been carefully executed, wherever possible by an artist from the country where the story originated, to reflect the culture and convey the full flavour of the story.

What more can be said? Let's share a story . . .

Jennie Ingham
29 January 1987

Jennie Ingham (BA MPhil) specializes in publishing dual language books and is the editor of the *Luzak Storytellers* series. She is a former Research Fellow in Education at Middlesex Polytechnic where she was a founder member of the *Reading Materials for Minority Groups* project. She has held several teaching and research posts and is a regular contributor to the *Times Educational Supplement*. She is a member of the United Kingdom Reading Association.

The Hare and the Tortoise

Retold by Gabriel Douloubakas

'What a lovely day,' said the hare, when he was crossing the field, and very happily he was licking his whiskers. And he said, 'Thank goodness, for once I am alone here with all these carrots, and no hunters after my life.'

He was strolling along singing to himself, and then he was eating the carrots one after the other, 'Chratts, chratts, chratts – I can eat as many carrots as I like for a whole year. An opportunity like this will never come again.'

When he was picking his last carrot he caught sight of the tortoise eating some grass.

The hare went up to the tortoise, thinking to himself, 'What have I got to fear from a tortoise?' And he said, 'What a nice day, my lovely friend.'

The tortoise answered, 'Yes, my dear hare, a very nice and peaceful day, not even a movement of a leaf.'

The hare jumped about happily and suddenly he said to the tortoise, 'I have a good idea.'

The tortoise said, 'I am listening, my dear hare.'

'What do you think about us two having a race?'

'You are very cunning, my dear hare,' and she was laughing loudly. 'Ha, ha, ha!'

But I am more cunning, she said to herself.

'Yes, I agree, but on one condition.'

Taken by surprise, the hare, who hadn't expected the tortoise to agree, said, 'Yes, whatever you say.'

'Well then, my hare, can you see that slope over there? What do you think of that for our race?'

'It's all right with me. Let's go,' he said happily.

I shall win, he said to himself.

They went to the edge of the slope to start the race. 'TSOUKOU TSOUKOU,' the tortoise was going.

I am surprised that she agreed to the race when she can't even walk, said the hare to himself.

When the tortoise caught up with the hare she said, 'Are you ready?'

'Of course I am ready, my dear tortoise. I am waiting for you,' and he was flapping his ears.

'Let's go,' the tortoise said – and she started rolling down the slope like a stone.

The hare was running as fast as he could but it was impossible to catch the tortoise.

In the middle of the slope the hare stopped and looked at the tortoise who was already at the finish.

The tortoise turned back and looked at the hare, who didn't think it was a fair race at all, and said, 'Where is your sense of humour? Shall we have another race?'

The Fisherman and the Jinnee

From The Arabian Nights

There was once a poor fisherman who lived by the sea. One day he went down to the sea shore as usual and cast his net into the water. Soon he felt something pulling at the net. The fisherman was delighted, thinking that he had caught a large fish, and he hauled in the net. But all he had caught was a dead donkey, so he threw it back into the sea and cast his net again with a prayer to Allah.

A few minutes later the fisherman again felt something inside his net and he pulled on the rope to draw in his catch. This time he found he'd caught nothing but a large, old broken jar filled with sand – not a fish in sight! When he cast his net for the third time he caught some pieces of old wood, seaweed and other rubbish! He *still* had nothing to eat for supper and nothing to sell at the market. Before he cast his net for the fourth and last time that day, he prayed to Allah that this time he might catch something worthwhile.

He threw his net into the sea and sat on the shore waiting. Then the net grew heavy, and the fisherman pulled and pulled until he had brought the net right up onto the sand.

There were still no fish, but inside the net was a large and rather interesting brass bottle with a lead stopper, sealed with the magic seal of the great Solomon himself.

Well, thought the fisherman, at least I could try selling this in the market – it might be worth a few pieces of gold. But he also decided that he would rather like to see what was inside the bottle, so he broke the seal with his knife and took out the lead stopper.

To his amazement, smoke began to pour from the mouth of the bottle, swirling along the ground and then up into the air, forming a thick black cloud above the fisherman's head. Gradually, from out of the smoke, a monstrous head began to take shape, and then a body and legs, and then hair and eyes and a mouth and a nose. There, standing before the fisherman, was a huge and terrifying Jinnee.

The poor fisherman fell to his knees and began to pray.

The Jinnee laughed. 'Prepare to meet your death, fisherman,' he roared.

The fisherman's knees knocked together, and he said in a small timid voice, 'But I let you out of the bottle, oh mighty Jinnee – I set you free. Why do you want to kill me?'

'I've been shut inside that bottle at the bottom of the sea for far too long to have any pity left,' said the Jinnee. 'You would understand if you knew my story.'

'Tell me your story, oh mighty Jinnee,' said the fisherman. 'I'd like to hear it before you kill me.'

'Many hundreds of years ago,' said the Jinnee, 'I disobeyed my master, Solomon the Great. To punish me, he put me inside this brass bottle, closed it with a lead stopper and sealed it with his magic seal. Then he had the bottle thrown into the deepest part of the ocean where it would never be found again. As I lay crushed inside the bottle, I swore for a hundred years that I would give anyone who set me free as much wealth, wisdom and happiness as he could ever want. Then, as another hundred years passed, I grew meaner and I decided I would only give him all the riches on earth.

'But no one ever came to free me and I rolled around in my bottle on the bottom of the sea for another four hundred years. After this time I grew very mean, for I decided that all I would give the person who freed me would be three wishes. And still no one came. Then I grew bitter and angry, and I swore I would kill the person who freed me. But I would still be a little kind, for I would let him choose how he wanted to die! Now, fisherman, choose!'

'L . . . l . . . let me ask you just one question,' said the fisherman.

'All right – but be quick about it,' growled the Jinnee.

'How could anyone as big as you fit into such a small bottle?' asked the fisherman. 'I just can't believe it can be done – you couldn't even fit your little toe into it.'

'So you don't believe me?' said the Jinnee.

'No,' said the fisherman, 'and I won't believe you until you prove that you can fit right inside the bottle.'

'Watch!' roared the Jinnee, and suddenly it had turned again into a whirling spiral of smoke, which disappeared in a flash into the bottle. Immediately the fisherman grabbed the bottle, put the stopper in, and fixed the seal firmly in place.

A howl came from inside the bottle. 'No, no, not again –

please set me free. I cannot bear to lie inside this bottle at the bottom of the sea for another thousand years.'

'Oh no,' said the fisherman, 'I shall throw you back into the sea where you belong, ungrateful one,' and he picked up the bottle and raised his arm as if he were going to throw the bottle out to sea.

'For the love of Allah, let me out,' cried the Jinnee, 'and I will give you as much wealth as you could ever desire.'

The fisherman made the Jinnee swear by Allah, Solomon, Mahomet and all the prophets that it wouldn't harm him, and finally he opened the bottle again.

Smoke poured from the bottle and the figure of the Jinnee took shape in the air.

Before the fisherman could say a word, the Jinnee kicked the bottle right out to sea — just to make sure the fisherman couldn't play any more tricks.

'Well, oh mighty Jinnee, you must now fulfil your part of the bargain,' said the fisherman.

The Jinnee laughed.

'Pick up your net, fisherman,' it said, 'and follow me.'

So the fisherman threw his net over his shoulder and followed the Jinnee through the mountains and across the desert until they came to a large lake. And when the fisherman looked into the water he saw that it was full of thousands and thousands of the strangest and most marvellous fish of every shape and colour.

'Throw your net into the water,' said the Jinnee, 'and then pull it in. Take four fish from it, each a different colour, and then throw the rest back into the lake. If you take your fish to the Sultan I swear that he will give you a great reward, and you and your family will have enough money to live on for many years. You can come back to the lake and catch more fish if you want to – but make sure you only cast your net once a day, and only ever take one fish of any colour at a time.'

'Now I have fulfilled my promise,' the Jinnee announced, 'I will leave you.' It stamped its foot and in an instant the ground opened and swallowed it up.

The fisherman was very pleased to have seen the last of the Jinnee and very pleased that his day had turned out so well. He took the fish to the Sultan and, as the Jinnee had said, he was given a magnificent reward, for the Sultan thought the fish were the most wonderful creatures he had ever seen.

And that night the fisherman and his family sat down to the best supper they had ever eaten.

The Enchanted Palace

Retold by Ashim Bhattacharya and Champaka Basu

Once upon a time there was a prince who was so handsome and good that he was greatly loved by everyone who knew him. He brought happiness to everybody and shone like a light throughout the kingdom.

One day the prince decided that he would travel to other countries outside his father's kingdom. All the subjects begged him not to leave them. The queen could not eat or sleep for worrying about him. Only the king gave his blessing.

A great many people organized themselves ready to accompany the prince. The queen brought him a tray full of jewels. But the prince would take nothing except a new suit of clothes and a shining new sword. Then he set off on his journey.

He walked on and on and on through many countries. He went over hills and mountains, through rivers and kingdoms, till finally he came to a forest.

Here no birds sang. Not a branch waved, not a leaf stirred, not an animal moved. He walked for many miles deep into the forest. Suddenly, he came upon a palace more beautiful

'Let's go,' the tortoise said
(*The Hare and the Tortoise*)

Suddenly he came upon a palace
(The Enchanted Palace)

'I want to eat you,' he said
(*The Crow and the Mango*)

There . . . was a huge and terrifying Jinnee
(The Fisherman and the Jinnee)

and magnificent than any he had ever seen. The tower at the palace gate touched the sky. The prince stood and gazed in admiration.

At the gate there was no sentry. In the tower no band played. Slowly the prince passed through the portals and into the palace. Everything was as clean as if it had been washed with milk. But all was still and silent. In the courtyard elephants, horses, guards and soldiers all lay in a deep sleep. In the armoury, where thousands of swords and bows and arrows hung upon the walls, soldiers and bodyguards stood unmoving, like statues made of stone. The prince shouted out his name, and asked to see the king, but only the echo of his own voice answered him. No one spoke. No one even looked at him.

In the grand durbar, a huge oil lamp cast its glow on a jewel-encrusted throne. But the king on his throne was a statue, his royal canopy askew. The court singers, prisoners, soldiers and guards all seemed to be carved from stone. No one even blinked.

Drawn by the scent of flowers, the prince wandered through the treasury, where clusters of lamps shone on piles of glittering diamonds and sparkling rubies. But the prince walked on, intoxicated by the fragrance.

As he entered the next room, he could see no pond, not even a drop of water, yet there were hundreds of thousands of lotus blossoms in full bloom. In the midst of this forest of flowers was a golden bed. The canopy was a garland of flowers. Beneath the garland was a golden lotus blossom on a diamond stalk, and fast asleep on the golden lotus was a beautiful princess. The prince gazed at her, overcome by her beauty. But neither her hands, nor her legs could be seen, only her pretty face, like moonshine, in the midst of the golden petals.

The prince was so entranced that years went by as he gazed at her without even a blink. Until, one day, he noticed on her pillow a golden stick. Moving forward quietly, he picked it up. No sooner had he done so than he saw, on the other side of the pillow, a silver stick. He held both the sticks in his hands, idly playing with them, and wondering where they had come from. And, while he did so, the gold stick fell on the princess's cheek.

All at once the blanket of lotus blossoms shivered, the golden bed gently shook, and the princess rubbed her eyes, stretched and woke up. As her hands and legs appeared, all the golden petals fell.

She gazed in wonder at the prince, for he had saved her.

And then she told him a strange story.

Many, many years ago, there was a terrible demon, who wanted the princess for himself. He captured her and, when she refused to marry him, he put a curse on her. The demon's grandmother, who was a witch, was left to guard her and the princess became the witch's slave. Every time she wished to be attended to, the witch used to wake up the princess with a golden stick. Gradually, she grew fond of the princess. The witch told her that the only way the curse could be removed was by killing the demon.

And the only way to kill the demon was to kill the bee which was trapped in a small box that lay in a crystal palace in the middle of a nearby lake. 'But', warned the princess, 'if one drop of blood falls on the ground then a thousand demons will come to life.'

Hearing this, the prince set forth at once. He found the lake and, in the middle, saw the crystal palace. Inside the palace he found the little box with the bee inside. He took the box outdoors and, over a pile of ashes, he killed the bee, so that not a drop of blood fell on the ground.

At once the curse was broken.

The birds around the palace started twittering, the sentries shouted orders, the horses neighed, the elephants trumpeted, and the soldiers stood to attention with a clatter. In the durbar, the king, his ministers and counsellors woke up. Everyone in the palace, wherever they were, awoke from a thousand years' sleep.

The prince, who, with his undying love and courage, had removed the curse, married the princess amidst great rejoicing. All around the palace, drums, shahnais and horns shouted the news. The people showered flowers and sprinkled chandan, and the flowers blossomed where they fell. A thousand drummers beat their drums and a royal feast was proclaimed. At this, hundreds upon hundreds of servants began preparing the spices, and thousands upon thousands began preparing the fish.

Then, in the gentle moonlight, before fire and a priest, the king attired the prince in a crown with five diamonds.

But, in his father's kingdom, there was nothing but gloom. Many years had passed since the prince had left on his journey. The king and queen and all the subjects wept for their lost prince, sure that he would now never return.

But suddenly, one day, the kingdom was awoken at dawn by sounds of great celebration. Everyone ran to the gates of the palace. And there what should they see but their beloved prince, leading in by the hand a beautiful princess.

Overcome by happiness, they welcomed the prince and his princess into their midst, and there they lived happily ever after.

The Crow and the Mango

Retold by Prapilla Mohanti

A crow was flying back home one day when he was attracted by a beautiful ripe mango.

'I want to eat you.' he said.

The mango replied, 'Go and wash your beak in the well and then you can eat me.'

The crow went to the well and said, 'Well, please give me some water so that I can wash my beak and eat the beautiful ripe mango.'

'There is no pot,' the well said; 'you must get one from the potter.'

So the crow went to the potter's house. 'Dear potter, please give me a pot so that I can get some water from the well to wash my beak and eat the beautiful ripe mango.'

The potter said, 'You must go and get me some clay so that I can make you a pot.'

The crow flew to the field and said, 'O field, please give me some clay so that the potter can make a pot for me to get some water from the well to wash my beak and eat the beautiful ripe mango.'

The field replied, 'Go to the deer and bring his horn so that you can dig out the clay.'

So the crow went to the deer. 'Please, deer, give me a horn to dig out the clay so that the potter can make a pot for me to get some water from the well to wash my beak and eat the beautiful ripe mango.'

The deer said, 'Bring me some milk from the black cow. I'll drink it first and then give you a horn.'

So the crow went to the cow and asked her, 'O cow, please give me milk for the deer to drink to give me his horn to dig out the clay for the potter to make a pot for me to get some water from the well to wash my beak and eat the beautiful ripe mango.'

'Get me some grass,' the black cow said. 'I'll give you milk when I eat it.'

The crow flew back to the field and said, 'Please give me grass for the black cow to eat to give milk for the deer to drink and give me his horn to dig out the clay for the potter to make a pot for me to get some water from the well to wash my beak and eat the beautiful ripe mango.'

'You must go to the blacksmith,' the field replied, 'and get a sickle to cut the grass.'

The crow went to the blacksmith and said, 'Please, black-smith, give me a sickle to cut the grass for the black cow to eat to give milk for the deer to drink and give me his horn to dig out the clay for the potter to make a pot for me to get some water from the well to wash my beak and eat the beautiful ripe mango.'

The blacksmith said, 'Wait a little, let me sharpen the

sickle.' So he put the sickle in the fire and when it was red hot he sharpened it. 'It's very hot, how will you carry it?'

By this time the crow was very impatient. 'Put it on my back,' he said.

The blacksmith did so, but the sickle was so hot that it burnt his feathers and after flying a few yards the crow dropped dead.

The beautiful ripe mango waited and waited patiently for the crow to come and eat it. But it became so ripe it fell to the ground.

Brer Anansi and the Ghost

Retold by David Makhanlall

For the past two weeks Brer Anansi couldn't get any sleep. It was not because he had slept during the day; Brer Anansi never slept during the day. Something had kept him awake.

It was a ghost!

At exactly twelve each night, he would scramble out of bed. It was always a wailing sound, to be heard at midnight. Then he would hear the clanking of chains. He would crawl to the crack in the window and fearfully peer out.

Outside, under and around his tree-house, he would see a ghost dancing about. It had on a white sheet and now and then it would leap into the air and give a horrible, cackling laugh.

Brer Anansi was haunted by a ghost!

He got Brer Weasel to stay one night thinking that the ghost wouldn't come. But the ghost came as usual and Brer Weasel left for home before the sun had risen. Brer Anansi had to sleep alone. Brer Weasel wouldn't have him in his house for fear that the ghost would follow.

Poor Brer Anansi. What a thing to have happened to him!

But he had no idea that his two enemies were behind it all. Brer Rabbit would wear a sheet, and his friend Brer Bear would drag rusty chains in the nearby bushes and do the howling. Brer Rabbit was good at dancing and Brer Bear was good at howling; what a good ghost they made!

For two weeks they had been scaring Brer Anansi nearly to death. Well, they had been scaring him for twelve nights, to be exact. Early in the morning after the twelfth scare, Brer Bear turned up at Brer Rabbit's burrow. They were going to discuss the following night's scaring.

'Operation Scare is proceeding well,' said Brer Rabbit. 'Brer Anansi must be wishing that he had never been born.'

'Serves him right!' exclaimed Brer Bear, helping himself to a slice of Brer Rabbit's toast. 'He deserves it. That will teach him not to interfere with us ever again.'

Brer Rabbit poured some coffee for Brer Bear.

'Yes, we will give him the final scare tonight. The thirteenth scare will be the last tonight, the best tonight, and the worst for Brer Anansi tonight!'

'Thirteen?' Brer Bear looked steadily at Brer Rabbit. 'That is a bad luck number.'

'Of course it is!' exclaimed his friend. 'Brer Anansi's bad luck tonight!'

'I am afraid.'

'You?' asked Brer Rabbit. 'Afraid? Don't be foolish. We are the ghost and Brer Anansi is the victim. We have nothing to be afraid of!'

'I hope so!'

Brer Rabbit handed his closest friend the plate of toast and poured him another cup of coffee.

'Here, you are worried over nothing! Eat up and let's go and prepare for tonight.'

Brer Anansi too had been thinking. He also realized that tonight would be the thirteenth night. He seemed to remember from somewhere that ghosts scare their victims for twelve nights and then attack them on the thirteenth.

He glanced at his calendar.

Today was Friday the thirteenth! His last day alive!

Brer Anansi couldn't eat. His breakfast lay untouched before him. He was sad. Very sad. He was going to die. He thought about his past life. It had been a happy life. He could remember the many times his two enemies had tricked him and the many more times he had tricked them. Indeed, he had tricked Brer Bear and Brer Rabbit so many times that he couldn't clearly remember the number.

He could remember when he had seemed as good as dead, yet he had always escaped. He had escaped!

Escaped?

Brer Anansi got up. He felt suddenly brave. He went in front of his mirror and looked at his reflection. There was a twinkle in his eyes.

'I, Brer Anansi,' he said, 'will not take things lying down. I have defeated Brer Rabbit and Brer Bear scores of times. I am going to defeat this ghost. Let him come tonight. Yes, let him come! Brer Anansi is not going to give up that easily. And I repeat: Brer Anansi is not going to give up that easily. Brer Anansi is going to defend his name!'

He sat down immediately and ate his breakfast with relish. Yes, he meant business. Brer Anansi was going to fight the ghost!

The night of Friday the thirteenth was a dark, cold night. There was no moon. What little light there was came from Brer Anansi's lamp up in his tree-house. It was ten o'clock. Brer Anansi was waiting for the ghost.

Meanwhile Brer Rabbit was practising his dance. Brer Bear felt cold and afraid. He didn't feel like going. Brer Rabbit stopped dancing.

'Why are you looking so afraid?'

'I am cold,' said Brer Bear. 'I don't feel well. I am afraid. Something is going to happen.'

'Stuff and nonsense!' exclaimed Brer Rabbit. 'Something is going to happen; not to us *but to Brer Anansi*. Stop looking so afraid.'

'What if a real ghost should come?'

'Nonsense!' shouted Brer Rabbit. 'A real ghost my back foot! Come on, help me with my sheet and let's go. Better early than late.'

Brer Bear was afraid. If a real ghost happened to come along, he reasoned, Brer Rabbit had the sheet and he might pass as a ghost too. He might escape. So Brer Bear took a sheet too. Brer Rabbit did not know this.

An hour later, the two friends came to the bushes near Brer Anansi's tree-house. They set about getting their equipment ready.

'You drag the chains as usual,' explained Brer Rabbit. 'I

will dance; but when it is exactly twelve, you set up the long ladder. I will climb, and give Brer Anansi the last and final shock in his life!'

Brer Bear nodded. He was still afraid that a real ghost might come.

At a quarter to twelve, the action started. Brer Rabbit danced and Brer Bear dragged the chains and howled. Brer Rabbit skipped around the tree-house five times. He paused a little next to the bush where Brer Bear was hiding.

'Go and set the ladder up!'

Brer Anansi waited, half afraid, half brave, up in his tree-house. He could see the ghost down below. But he too had his secret weapons ready! He was waiting for the correct time.

Brer Rabbit went around the tree-house. When he was out of sight, Brer Bear put on his white sheet. He got up to go and fetch the ladder leaning against a nearby tree.

Just then Brer Rabbit came out from around the corner of the house, dancing away, eyes closed. Brer Bear was looking behind. They did not see each other! When they were a yard apart, Brer Rabbit opened his eyes. Just then Brer Bear looked in front.

They both stared. *Two ghosts*!

Brer Bear thought that the white sheet in front of him was the ghost.

Brer Rabbit, at the same time, thought that the white sheet in front of *him* was the real ghost Brer Bear had asked him about.

Both friends screamed and turned abruptly around to try to escape.

Just then, Brer Anansi put his first secret plan into action! He thought he saw the ghost stop. Indeed, his two enemies were standing right in the noose of his long rope. Just as they both screamed and turned to go, Brer Anansi pulled his rope! Both friends were caught by a leg each. There they dangled, one from the left leg, one from the right leg, at the end of a rope some ten feet above the ground. How they each struggled! The sheets had fallen off but the place was so dark they couldn't see properly. How they fought!

Then Brer Anansi put his number two secret plan into action.

He put on his white sheet and raced down his silk rope, howling away. At the bottom he stopped. Was it Brer Bear and Brer Rabbit dangling at the end of the rope?

He came closer and looked. Indeed it was. Brer Anansi smiled; they had been the 'ghost' after all. Ah. What fun he was going to get now!

Brer Anansi held his sheet tighter around himself and howled towards the two friends dangling from the rope. They both stopped fighting and looked down. What a shock!

There was a third ghost coming at them! They began to struggle afresh to escape. Brer Anansi howled closer and closer, his many feet doing a perfect ballet dance.

Then the rope broke!

Both friends went down and managed to find their feet. They both howled and ran out into the cold, dark night. Brer Anansi watched them go.

'Ha,' he said, 'that really took care of you two rogues!'

He took up the two fallen white sheets and went up his silk rope.

'You won't need white sheets again,' he said, as he climbed up. 'I can bet that Brer Rabbit and Brer Bear won't want to see a white sheet ever again!'

Brer Anansi and the Rainbow's End

Retold by David Makhanlall

One bright April morning Brer Anansi saw the most beautiful rainbow in the world. At least *he* thought that it was the most beautiful rainbow in the world. It had all the possible colours he could think of – blue, red, green, yellow and many others. The rainbow was simply beautiful.

Brer Anansi scratched his head and looked again at the rainbow. Now I seem to remember some tale, he said to himself, that rainbows have a pot of gold at one end. It might be true, he decided, so I will go and look for it. But first I have to prepare a meal as it might be a very long journey.

After Brer Anansi had tied up a meal in a handkerchief and tied it to the end of a stick, he set off on his search for the pot of gold. He had hardly covered half a mile when he met Brer Buzzard.

'Where are you off to, Brer Anansi?' asked Brer Buzzard.

'I am off to the end of the rainbow,' replied Brer Anansi, looking up at the big, beautiful rainbow.

'To the end of the rainbow?' repeated Brer Buzzard. 'But

that is a very long journey. I have often tried flying there but there seems to be no end to that colourful band in the skies. What are you going there for, by the way?'

Brer Anansi was not stupid. He knew that if he told Brer Buzzard, the bird would follow him; he could fly faster and might reach the end of the rainbow first and collect all the gold.

'Oh,' replied Brer Anansi carelessly, 'I feel like taking a long walk today so I have decided to follow the rainbow. Care to come along?'

'Oh, no! Not me!' replied Brer Buzzard, shaking his head. 'I would never get there even if I flew for a year.'

Brer Anansi was left to continue his journey alone. All the better, for he wanted the gold for himself. Brer Buzzard was flying homewards when he saw Brer Bear taking his morning stroll. He flew down, keeping well out of reach, and said, 'You know what, Brer Bear? Brer Anansi is on his way to the end of the rainbow. He says he needs a lot of exercise today.'

'Who cares where he is going to?' replied Brer Bear. 'If he wants to go to the end of the rainbow, let him go!'

After Brer Buzzard had flown away, Brer Bear scratched his head. I seem to remember, he thought, some story about the rainbow. Wait, I remember now! There is a pot of gold at the end. So that's what Brer Anansi is after, but not if I can help it! Brer Bear followed quickly after Brer Anansi. He too wanted the gold.

Meanwhile, Brer Buzzard met Brer Rabbit. He kept well out of Brer Rabbit's reach because he knew that if Brer Rabbit got hold of him he would pull out all his feathers,

The two friends came to the bushes
(Brer Anansi and the Ghost)

'Who's that running, trit-trot, trit-trot. . .'
(*The Three Billy Goats Gruff*)

'Come with me,' said Fox Lox
(*Chicken Licken*)

He followed them
(*Brer Anansi and the Rainbow's End*)

one by one, by way of repaying all the ill deeds that he had done to Brer Rabbit in the past.

'Brer Rabbit, Brer Anansi is off to the end of the rainbow, and so is Brer Bear.'

Brer Rabbit picked up a stone and threw it at Brer Buzzard. 'Off with you! I don't need you around. Mischief maker!'

Brer Rabbit was smart. After Brer Buzzard had disappeared among the trees, he followed Brer Bear. He knew that since Brer Bear was following Brer Anansi, something was up, and he wanted to know what.

The three adventurers were off to the end of the rainbow. Brer Anansi was about two miles ahead of Brer Bear and Brer Rabbit brought up the rear. They had been travelling for ten minutes when Brer Anansi became tired. He wanted to rest. The sun was rising higher in the sky and it was very hot. Brer Anansi climbed up a tree where the blowing leaves made him feel cooler. He soon became too comfortable to move and decided to stay up there awhile.

Brer Bear saw Brer Anansi go into the woods, still following the rainbow, so he followed after. But when he came to the woods, there was no sign of Brer Anansi at all.

'Where can he have gone to?' said Brer Bear, looking around. He sat under a tree and decided to rest a little and then go and look for Brer Anansi. Without knowing it he had sat under the same tree that Brer Anansi was in. Brer Anansi kept very still. He didn't want Brer Bear to know that he was up there as he might follow him when he resumed his journey. He did not know that Brer Bear had been following him for some time now.

Brer Rabbit, seeing Brer Bear go into the woods too, followed him in. He thought that Brer Bear would be walking after Brer Anansi but when he came to the clearing in the woods, he saw Brer Bear sitting under a tree.

Brer Bear got quite excited when he saw Brer Rabbit. 'What are you doing here?' asked Brer Bear.

'Oh, I saw you coming in here all stealthy-like so I decided to follow you,' replied Brer Rabbit.

'I was following Brer Anansi and he seems to have disappeared,' explained Brer Bear.

'I wonder where he could have gone to,' said Brer Rabbit. 'He could not have gone to the end of the rainbow without our seeing him.'

Brer Anansi stood perfectly still on a branch of the tree. So, his two enemies had followed him. The two wanted the gold for themselves, thought Brer Anansi. He listened to what the two were saying.

'I know what we should do,' said Brer Bear. 'You go and look for him over there and I will look over this side of the tree. Shout and call me if you find him, and I will do the same if I find him before you.'

So the two separated. Each went in opposite directions. Brer Anansi watched as they disappeared noisily into the bushes. Soon the sound grew further and further away. Finally, there was silence. Brer Anansi came down from his tree and ate his snack. He was soon finished and climbed up the tree again.

Half an hour later, Brer Rabbit and Brer Bear returned. They were both tired out and hungry. Their hides were inflamed and bruised where the thorns had pricked them. Brer Bear had a big bump on his nose where a bee had stung him.

'If ever I get my hands on that Brer Anansi, he'll be sorry that he tried to go to the end of the rainbow!' said Brer Bear, rubbing the end of his nose. How it pained him!

Brer Rabbit too was very, very angry. He had been scratched and bitten by all sorts of insects. He had even encountered bugs when he crawled under a rotten tree trunk to see if Brer Anansi was under it. Bats flew at him when he entered a cave.

'Let's take a bath,' said Brer Bear. 'It may help to cure our pains. But I can assure you that Brer Anansi will never cure his when I'm finished with him!'

The two friends disappeared into the bushes and Brer Anansi slid down from the tree. He followed them and saw them take off their clothes and plunge into a pool. He crawled quietly up to their clothes, took them away and proceeded to rub some itch-bushes on them.

'That will teach them not to follow me about,' he said. 'I would have had the pot of gold already if they had kept away from the tree when I wanted to come down. Nosey idiots!'

Then he took the clothes back to the side of the pond and ran home. He took a pot from his kitchen cupboard and filled it to the brim with stones.

He went back to the pond and looked down at the two animals thrashing about in the water.

'Oh, my poor feet! This is worse,' said Brer Rabbit, almost in tears. 'I am still in pain.'

'If ever I get my hands on Brer Anansi!' said Brer Bear, and smacked his fists together.

'Is that so?' asked Brer Anansi. 'What have I done to deserve such treatment, you rogues!'

As soon as the two friends saw Brer Anansi, they roared together:

'There he is! After him! Tar his black furry skin! Never mind the gold in the pot. Don't let him get away!'

Quickly they clambered out of the water and put on their clothes. They were in such a hurry that they failed to notice the green, itchy leaves on their clothes.

Meanwhile Brer Anansi was off like a shot! He ran as fast as he could with his pot of stones. The two friends ran quickly after him as soon as they got their clothes on. They were catching up with Brer Anansi who could not run very fast with his pot of stones. But he didn't have to worry.

Brer Rabbit was a few yards behind Brer Anansi when he felt very funny. Something was tickling him. Then he felt itchy all over and scratched away as fast as he could. How he itched!

Brer Bear was amazed. He was a few yards behind and saw his friend stop abruptly and scratch furiously. What is wrong with him, said Brer Bear to himself. He soon found out, for he too began feeling itchy. How he itched. The two friends were scratching away as fast as they could!

Brer Anansi laughed and laughed. It was great fun to see his two enemies scratching away like mad.

'Serves you right, Brer Bear, for following me, and you too, Brer Rabbit. In future, mind your own business!'

Brer Anansi ran home when he thought the itching was beginning to wear off. He had to be far away when his two enemies recovered. I will go and look for the gold another time, thought Brer Anansi, if Brer Rabbit and Brer Bear ever let me alone.

The Three Billy Goats Gruff

Traditional

Three goats once lived together in a field. The littlest one was called Little Billy Goat Gruff. The next one was bigger than Little Billy Goat Gruff, so he was called Big Billy Goat Gruff. But the third was the biggest of them all, and he was called Great Big Billy Goat Gruff.

At the end of their field was a river, and across the river was another field. Now this field was empty and the grass there grew rich and long and very green. Little Billy Goat Gruff said he could see some beautiful rosy apples on a tree over in the field. Big Billy Goat Gruff said there was plenty of lovely clover there. And Great Big Billy Goat Gruff said he had seen ripe red berries growing there as well. They all longed to cross the river.

There was a low bridge that crossed the river between the two fields, but under it there lived a horrible troll who liked to eat goats better than anything else. So the three Billy Goats Gruff never dared to cross the bridge into the lovely empty field in case the troll caught them.

One day Little Billy Goat Gruff felt very, very hungry and

he told his brothers: 'I'm going to cross over the bridge and eat some of those rosy apples.'

His brothers said, 'Be careful; remember the troll. He's certain to catch you.'

But Little Billy Goat Gruff was determined. Off he went, trit-trot, trit-trot, over the bridge. 'I'm too small for him,' he said.

When he was half-way across the bridge, the troll suddenly put his head out and said, 'Who's that running, trit-trot, trit-trot, over my bridge?'

'It's only me, Little Billy Goat Gruff.'

'I'm going to eat you up,' said the troll.

But Little Billy Goat Gruff said, 'Don't eat me, because I'm only *Little* Billy Goat Gruff. I've got a brother called *Big* Billy Goat Gruff, who is much bigger and fatter than I am. Why don't you wait for him?'

'All right,' growled the troll, 'I will.'

So Little Billy Goat Gruff trotted across the bridge to the other field and began to eat all the long green grass and the beautiful rosy apples.

Big Billy Goat Gruff saw that Little Billy Goat Gruff had got safely across; so off he went too, trit-trot, trit-trot, over the bridge.

When he was half-way across, the troll put his head out and said, 'Who's that running, trit-trot, trit-trot, over my bridge?'

'It's only Big Billy Goat Gruff.'

'Then I'm going to eat you up,' growled the troll.

But Big Billy Goat Gruff said, 'Don't eat me, because I'm

only *Big* Billy Goat Gruff. I've got a brother called *Great* Big Billy Goat Gruff, who is still bigger and fatter than I am. Why don't you wait for him?'

'All right,' grunted the troll, 'I will.'

So Big Billy Goat Gruff trotted across the bridge to the other side and began to feast on the long green grass and the lovely clover.

Great Big Billy Goat Gruff thought it was time he went over to join his brothers and have some of the long green grass and the ripe red berries. So off he went, trit-trot, trit-trot, over the bridge. When he was half-way across, the troll put out his head and said, 'Who's that running, trit-trot, trit-trot, over my bridge.'

'It's Great Big Billy Goat Gruff.'

'You're the one I'm going to gobble up,' growled the troll. 'I've been waiting for you.'

Trying not to look frightened, Great Big Billy Goat Gruff said, 'Oh have you? You just try to gobble me up and see what happens.'

Then the troll jumped up onto the bridge, but Great Big Billy Goat Gruff put down his head, ran at the troll and knocked him off the bridge and into the river. The troll disappeared howling under the water and was drowned.

Great Big Billy Goat Gruff trotted across the bridge to the other side and joined Big Billy Goat Gruff and Little Billy Goat Gruff in their new field. They all ate the long green grass, and Great Big Billy Goat Gruff ate the ripe red berries, Big Billy Goat Gruff ate the lovely clover, and Little Billy Goat Gruff ate all the beautiful rosy apples. And they all grew very fat.

Chicken Licken

Traditional

As Chicken Licken was in the wood one day, an acorn fell from a tree onto his poor bald head.

'Oh dear,' he thought. 'The sky is falling! I must go and tell the king.'

So he left the wood and on the way he met Hen Len. 'Well, Hen Len,' he said, 'where are you going?'

'I'm going to the wood,' said Hen Len.

'Oh don't go there,' said Chicken Licken, 'for I was there and the sky fell on my poor bald head, and I'm going to tell the king.'

'Can I come with you?' said Hen Len.

'Certainly,' said Chicken Licken.

So off they went together to tell the king the sky was falling.

As they travelled along they met Cock Lock. 'Well, Cock Lock,' said Hen Len, 'where are you going?'

'I'm going to the wood,' said Cock Lock.

'Oh, Cock Lock, don't go there,' said Hen Len, 'for Chicken Licken was there and the sky fell on his poor bald head and we're going to tell the king.'

'May I come with you?' said Cock Lock.

'Certainly,' said Chicken Licken.

So off they all went together to tell the king the sky was falling.

As they travelled onwards they met Duck Luck. 'Well, Duck Luck,' said Cock Lock, 'where are you going?'

'I'm going to the wood,' said Duck Luck.

'Oh, Duck Luck, don't go there,' said Cock Lock, 'for Chicken Licken was there and the sky fell on his poor bald head and we're going to tell the king.'

'May I come with you?' said Duck Luck.

'Of course,' said Chicken Licken, and so off they all went together to tell the king the sky was falling.

As they travelled on, they met Drake Lake. 'Well, Drake Lake,' said Duck Luck, 'where are you going?'

'I'm going to the wood,' said Drake Lake.

'Oh, Drake Lake, don't go there,' said Duck Luck, 'for Chicken Licken was there and the sky fell on his poor bald head and we're going to tell the king.'

'May I come with you?' said Drake Lake.

'Of course,' said Chicken Licken, and off they all went together to tell the king the sky was falling.

On they travelled until they met Goose Loose. 'Well, Goose Loose,' said Drake Lake, 'where are you going?'

'I'm going to the wood,' said Goose Loose.

'Oh, Goose Loose, don't go there,' said Drake Lake, 'for Chicken Licken was there and the sky fell on his poor bald head, and we're going to tell the king.'

'May I come with you?' said Goose Loose.

'Certainly,' said Chicken Licken, and off they all went to tell the king the sky was falling.

On their way they met Turkey Lurkey. 'Well, Turkey Lurkey,' said Goose Loose, 'where are you going?'

'I'm going to the wood,' said Turkey Lurkey.

'Oh, Turkey Lurkey, don't go there,' said Goose Loose, 'for Chicken Licken was there and the sky fell on his poor bald head and we're off to tell the king.'

'May I come with you?' said Turkey Lurkey.

'Of course,' said Chicken Licken, and off they all went to tell the king the sky was falling.

As they travelled onwards they met Fox Lox. And Fox Lox said, 'Where are you going?'

'Chicken Licken was in the wood and the sky fell on his poor bald head,' said all the birds together, 'and we're going to tell the king.'

'Come with me,' said Fox Lox, 'and I will show you the way. The king will be delighted to see you.'

They all followed him until they came to a dark, dark hole in the edge of the hillside. 'This is the way to the king,' said Fox Lox. So in went Chicken Licken, Hen Len, Cock Lock, Duck Luck, Drake Lake, Goose Loose and Turkey Lurkey, one after the other. But this was not the way to the king's palace, it was Fox Lox's den. And in no time at all Fox Lox had gobbled up every one of them, so they never saw the king to tell him that the sky was falling.

The Willow-Leaf Eyebrow

Retold by Sonia Roetter

Once upon a time there lived the maiden Chen Lien, who was as graceful as a willow branch and as beautiful as a statue carved of milk-white jade. But there was one thing that spoiled her beauty: her left eyebrow was cut by a scar from an accident that had befallen her when she was a child.

One day a handsome and rich young man named Wu Fang was climbing in the trees near Chen Lien's home, looking for birds' nests, when he happened to look down over her father's wall, and saw the young lady sewing in her garden. Her good eyebrow was towards him, and so he thought her the most beautiful girl he had ever seen. The more he looked and the more he thought about her the more he knew he was in love, so that night he begged his parents to arrange for his marriage to the girl in the garden. He begged them so pitifully that they consented.

They sent for a matchmaker of the neighbourhood, and after many gifts and many journeys back and forth the marriage was arranged. But the matchmaker said to Wu

Fang: 'The young maiden is good, she is rich, and she is beautiful. Still, there is one flaw in her beauty, and you should know about it before you go ahead and finish all the arrangements.'

'I have seen the young woman, and I know her beauty,' said the young man, and would listen no further.

Finally the day of the wedding ceremony arrived, and the courtyard of Chen Lien's home was heaped with wedding gifts from near and far. But still the bride was sad, for she feared that her husband would be terribly angry and disappointed when he first saw her bad eyebrow.

But her mother comforted her, saying: 'I am sure the matchmaker has told the young man about your eyebrow, and he wants you in spite of it.' But still the bride was unhappy, even at the wedding, as she looked through her heavy veil and saw her handsome new husband laughing and smiling among the feasting guests.

But finally the ceremonies and the feastings were over and the guests went home, and the time came for the groom to lift the veil from the face of his bride – and who can blame him if he seemed to start in surprise when he saw the imperfect eyebrow?

Poor Chen Lien saw the surprise on her husband's face, and she said: 'Good husband, did not the matchmaker tell you of my bad eyebrow? It was injured when I was a little girl. I was visiting distant friends with my parents, and I was playing in their garden. A little boy in the garden threw a heavy stone. I am sure that he did not wish to hurt me, but it hit me on the forehead, and cut this gash which you see. I am sorry that I cannot come to you, my husband, perfect in every way.'

'O Lady of Sweetness,' said Wu Fang, 'what was the name of that little boy who threw the stone?'

'Alas, I do not know; he was a visitor there like myself.'

'Was the garden in which you were playing that of the Li family in the city of Peking?' asked Wu gently.

'O excellent husband, how could you know that?'

'Because that boy was myself,' said Wu. 'My parents have often told me how I threw a stone and cut the forehead of a little girl in the gardens of the Lis. The good gods themselves must have arranged to tie our ankles with the silken cord of marriage, so that I might make amends to you for the injury I caused. And now I know what I must do.'

Then he called for the finest black ink and his thinnest and best writing-brush, and with the brush and the ink he drew a new eyebrow right through the scar. It was thin and curved, like a willow leaf, and it was so like Chen Lien's perfect eyebrow that no one could tell them apart. And for all the many happy years that the two lovers lived together, every morning husband Wu Fang painted a new willow-leaf eyebrow over the scar which he had made.

Ko-ai and her Lost Shoe

Retold by Sonia Roetter

In the ancient city of Peking there are two mighty towers set in the outer wall. One is called the Drum Tower. There the tower-keeper had a water clock, and, as each hour dripped away, he would pound his drum, so the people could learn the time. The other tower is called the Bell Tower. Each morning when it was time for the gates to be opened, and each night when it was time for the gates to be closed, the tower-keeper used to strike the great bell which hung there, and for miles around you could hear its deep 'Booooom-m-m'. And if all was still, and if you listened very carefully, you could hear also a faint delicate note 'Shhhieh-h-h-h', which the people said was the whisper of Ko-ai, calling for her lost shoe.

These towers were built in ancient times as watch-towers, and the emperor of that time, a proud man, was determined to have the largest towers in China, and the loudest drum, and finest bell. 'For the bell,' he said, 'we must find the finest bell-maker in China. He must use iron for strength, and brass for loudness, and gold for mellowness, and silver for sweetness.'

So this proud emperor gave orders to his chamberlains to get all of these metals gathered together, and he gave orders to all the governors of all the provinces to send to Peking the most skilful bell-makers from their particular province.

When all the metals had been gathered, and all the bell-makers were come, great fires were started to melt the metals, and for many days there was much stirring, and mixing, and testing. At last the metal was ready to be poured into the bell-mould, and the emperor and all his court gathered to watch the casting of the great bell. As music played and ladies fluttered their fans, the heavy pots of flowing metal were poured into the mould till it was filled to the very top; and then, because it would be many hours before the metal cooled, all the court went away again, while the master bell-maker, Kuan Yu, watched over the bell alone with his assistants.

But alas! Many hours later, when the metal was cool, Kuan Yu broke away the clay of the mould, and saw that the metal of the new bell was full of holes and flaws.

The emperor was notified, and was much annoyed. A great deal of time and money had been wasted. But he told Kuan Yu to try again; and again the metals were gathered, were mixed with even greater care, and were poured into a new mould with the greatest precautions. Only a few of the court came to watch the pouring of the metal, and Kuan Yu was soon left alone with his bell. And again, after the metal cooled, he found that the bell was imperfect.

This time the emperor was very angry. He gave Kuan Yu one more chance. 'Next time,' said he, 'I am richer by a

He drew a new eyebrow
(*The Willow-Leaf Eyebrow*)

Hansel was kept in his cage
(*Hansel and Gretel*)

'Apples, lovely apples,' she cried
(Snow White and the Seven Dwarfs)

Ko-ai calling for her lost shoe
(*Ko-ai and Her Lost Shoe*)

perfect bell, or *you* are poorer by a head!' The poor bell-maker went home full of sadness and despair.

Kuan Yu's daughter, Ko-ai, was a lovely girl of fifteen. She was the bell-maker's only child, and he loved her dearly, as she loved him. When he came home so sad because of the emperor's anger, she did her best to cheer him up. She told him that the gods could help him; she promised him that his third try would make a world's wonder of a bell; but Kuan Yu would not be cheered. He made his plans for the third bell-casting with a heavy heart indeed.

Ko-ai was worried about the bell, so she went to a fortune-teller. This fortune-teller listened gravely to her story, consulted his beads and books, and wrote down a poem, which he told her to read at midnight. This was the poem:

The warring metals celebrate their union.
They pass the goblet: lo, a maiden's blood!

You can imagine with what trembling poor Ko-ai read this poem, for it could have only one meaning: a maiden's blood would have to be added to the molten metals, or they would never fuse together properly to make a fine bell. And what maiden other than her poor self could be meant?

She cried all night long, but in the morning she bravely wiped her eyes and went to her father to beg his permission to be present at the third casting of the bell.

When the day came, Ko-ai was in the crowd with her old nurse. There was a great crowd, for everyone at court knew that Kuan Yu would lose his life if this bell were not perfect.

Once again the cauldrons of carefully blended molten

metal flowed into the great bell-mould, once again the musicians played and the ladies fluttered their fans. But just as the largest cauldron was being emptied, the lovely Ko-ai ran to the edge of the bell-mould. 'I do this for thee, O good father!' she said as she ran, and with one quick backward glance she leaped into the molten metal.

Everyone cried and shrieked. The musicians stopped playing. Even the emperor turned pale. The molten metal bubbled up in bright colours for a moment, and then it settled slowly and smoothly into the mould again. But there was nothing to be seen of Ko-ai except one little shoe, which her old nurse still held in her hand, for she had rushed forward to catch her as she jumped.

The fortune-teller had been right. Many hours later, when the bell-mould was broken open, the metal was seen to be flawless, and when it was hung up and tested, the bell was louder and more beautiful than any that had ever before been heard or seen in China. Its loud 'Booooom-m-m!' could be heard across the miles, and after each great note came a whispering 'Shhhieh-h-h' which people said was poor Ko-ai calling for her lost shoe.

Hansel and Gretel

Brothers Grimm

There was once a poor woodcutter who had scarcely enough money to feed his wife and his two children.

One night his wife said, 'Listen to me. We can't afford to keep our children any longer. Tomorrow morning you must give them each a piece of bread and take them into the forest. Build them a fire to keep them warm and then leave them to look after themselves.'

The two children, Hansel and Gretel, were lying awake in their beds and heard everything their mother said. They were terrified; but suddenly Hansel had an idea. He crept out of the front door and collected some of the white pebbles that lay on the path. He put them in his coat pocket and then went back to bed.

Early the next morning the woodcutter took Hansel and Gretel into the heart of the forest, first giving them each a piece of bread. As they walked, Hansel dropped the little white pebbles, one by one, along the way.

When they reached a clearing in the part of the forest where the trees were thickest and darkest, the woodcutter built a fire. 'Sit here,' he said. 'Warm yourselves by the fire and eat your bread. I'm off to cut down trees but I'll be back for you before dark.'

The children sat by the fire all day, but by sunset they knew that their father would not be coming back for them. However, when night fell and the moon rose, the path of white pebbles Hansel had dropped gleamed in the moonlight, and the two children followed them all the way home.

The woodcutter was secretly delighted that his children had returned, but his wife was not going to give up so easily and told him that he would have to take them back into the forest the next day. That night she locked the children in their room so that Hansel could not collect any more pebbles.

The next day the woodcutter gave Hansel and Gretel a piece of bread as before and took them into the heart of the forest. As they walked, Hansel dropped breadcrumbs on the path, but when night fell and the moon came up there was nothing to be seen, for all the crumbs of bread had been eaten by the birds of the forest.

Hansel and Gretel wandered in the forest for three days. On the third day, however, they came across a little hut made of gingerbread, with a roof made of cake and icing, and windows made of sweets and barley sugar. 'Now there is more than enough for us to eat,' said Gretel. 'You eat the roof, Hansel, and I'll eat the windows and then the walls.'

As Gretel broke a piece of barley sugar from the window, they heard a voice from inside the house.

'Tip, tap – who is it?'

'It's only the wind blowing through the trees,' Gretel answered.

Suddenly the door of the house opened and out came a shrivelled old woman. Hansel and Gretel were very frightened, but the old woman said kindly, 'Come in, come in — there's plenty for you to eat inside.'

She led them into the house and gave them both an enormous meal. Then she showed them two neat little beds, and soon the children were tucked up and fast asleep. But in the night the old woman took Hansel away and locked him in a cage. For she was really a wicked witch, and there was nothing she liked better than eating children, provided they were fat enough.

From that moment she made Gretel work hard in the house, while Hansel was kept in his cage and fed ten large meals a day. Every day the witch would poke him to see if he was plump enough to eat.

One day the witch decided that Hansel was just right for her supper, and she told Gretel to light a fire in the oven and lay the table. Gretel lit the oven as she was told and watched the flames grow higher and higher.

'Is it hot enough yet?' snapped the witch. 'Put your head inside and see.' Gretel pretended to look inside the oven.

'I'm not sure,' she said. 'Perhaps you'd better have a look.'

The witch bent down and put her head inside the oven. Suddenly Gretel pushed her from behind and — *crash!* — with a scream she fell right inside. Gretel slammed the oven door shut and that was the end of the witch.

Gretel then opened the door of the cage and let Hansel

out. 'Come on,' she said. 'I know where the witch kept her store of gold and jewels.' She took Hansel to a chest filled with diamonds, pearls, rubies, sapphires, gold and silver, and the two children filled their pockets, Then they set out for home.

After many days wandering in the forest they finally found the path that led them back to the woodcutter's cottage.

When the two children emptied their pockets of the witch's treasure, the woodcutter and his wife could hardly believe their eyes — but they knew that for the rest of their lives they would never have to worry again about being able to buy a loaf of bread.

Snow White and the Seven Dwarfs

Brothers Grimm

One winter's day as the snow was falling, a queen was sewing at her window. As she was looking out she pricked her finger and three drops of blood fell onto the snow. The queen said to herself, 'I wish my little daughter had skin as white as the snow, lips and cheeks as red as the drops of my blood, and hair as black as the ebony of the window frame.'

And her little girl grew up with snow-white skin, rose-red lips and beautiful black hair, and she was called Snow White.

The queen died, and the king married another wife, who was very beautiful, but so proud that she could not bear to think that anyone was lovelier than she. The new queen had a magic looking-glass, which always spoke the truth, and the queen used to look at herself in it and say:

> Mirror, mirror, on the wall,
> Who is the fairest of us all?

And the glass always used to say:

Queen, you are the fairest in the land.

As Snow White grew older, she became more and more beautiful. One day when the queen looked in the mirror and said:

Mirror, mirror, on the wall,
Who is the fairest of us all?

the glass answered:

Queen, how fair and beautiful you are!
But Snow White is more beautiful by far.

The queen turned pale with fury and, calling one of her servants, she said, 'Take Snow White away into the forest and kill her.'

The servant took Snow White away, but he could not bear to kill her and instead left her to wander in the forest.

Just as night was falling, Snow White came to a little cottage. Inside were seven chairs drawn up to a table, which was laid with seven little plates, seven glasses, seven knives and seven forks. By the wall stood seven beds.

Snow White was so tired that she lay down on a bed and fell fast asleep. Presently, in came the seven dwarfs who lived in the cottage. They lit their seven lamps and at once they saw Snow White lying on the bed.

'What a lovely child she is!' they all said.

In the morning Snow White told the dwarfs her story. They said she could stay in the cottage with them and they would look after her. But every day when they set off for work, digging in the gold mines of the mountains, they warned her not to let anyone in.

The queen, thinking now that Snow White was dead, asked her glass:

> Mirror, mirror, on the wall,
> Who is the fairest of us all?

And the glass said:

> Snow White in the forest green
> Is far the loveliest, O Queen.

The queen was furious, as she knew that her servant had betrayed her. She disguised herself as an old woman and set off into the forest. Soon she came to the dwarfs' cottage, and saw Snow White inside. She knocked at the door, calling: 'Laces to sell: Laces to sell!'

Snow White peeped out of the window and, seeing only a poor old woman, she opened the door and bought some laces.

'Let me lace your dress for you,' said the queen. But she pulled the laces so tight that Snow White fell to the ground as if she were dead. And then the queen went home, cackling with laughter.

The seven dwarfs came back that evening and found Snow White lying on the ground. They immediately cut the laces and she began to breathe again. When they heard what had happened they said, 'That old woman was the wicked queen. You must be more careful. Don't let anyone in again.'

The queen arrived back at her castle and went straight to her glass:

> Mirror, mirror, on the wall,
> Who is the fairest of us all?

To her horror the mirror replied:

> Snow White in the forest green
> Is far the loveliest, O Queen.

The queen knew that her plan had failed, so she disguised herself as a comb seller and took a basket of poisoned combs to the dwarfs' cottage. She knocked at the door, but Snow White answered: 'I'm sorry, but I'm not letting anyone in.'

'There's no need to,' said the queen. 'You can look at my combs through the window.'

Snow White looked at the combs. They were so beautiful that she took one and put it in her hair; but as soon as the poisoned comb touched her head she fell to the ground as if she were dead. And the queen went back to her castle.

When they got home that evening the dwarfs guessed what had happened. As soon as they took the comb from Snow White's hair, she woke up. The dwarfs repeated their warnings against the queen's evil tricks.

On reaching her castle, the wicked queen went straight to her glass:

> Mirror, mirror, on the wall,
> Who is the fairest of us all?

The glass replied:

> Snow White in the forest green
> Is far the loveliest, O Queen.

The queen turned away in fury, and, dressing herself as a country woman, she set off for the dwarfs' cottage with a basket of apples. One of the apples was especially beautiful — red on one side and green on the other. But the red part was poisoned.

The queen knocked at the door. 'Apples, lovely apples,' she cried.

'I do not want to buy them,' said Snow White.

'Just try one,' said the queen. 'Share it with me,' and she took a bite from the green half of the poisoned apple.

This apple must be safe if the woman is eating it herself, thought Snow White. She reached out for the apple and took a bite from the red half. Immediately she fell to the ground and her breathing stopped.

Certain that this time she had been successful, the evil queen hurried home. When she reached her castle again she spoke to her glass:

> Mirror, mirror, on the wall,
> Who is the fairest of us all?

This time the glass answered:

> O Queen, you are the fairest in the land.

At last the wicked queen was happy.

When the dwarfs returned they thought that this time

Snow White was dead. They wept and mourned for three days, and then they laid her in a coffin of glass and placed it on a hillside, so that her beauty could still be seen.

Many years later a handsome prince was riding by and saw the lovely girl lying in the coffin. He lifted her in his arms and the piece of poisoned apple fell from Snow White's mouth.

Immediately she awoke and fell in love with the prince as he had already fallen in love with her. The prince asked Snow White to marry him and she happily agreed.

On their wedding day, as the wicked queen stood in front of her glass and said:

> Mirror, mirror, on the wall,
> Who is the fairest of us all?

it answered to her horror:

> O Queen, how fair and beautiful you are!
> But Snow White, the prince's bride is lovelier by far.

The queen was so angry she died in a fit of rage. But Snow White and her prince lived happily ever after.

The Loving Dog

Retold by Lafcadio Hearn

Once there were an old man and his wife who lived alone on their little farm, all alone except for their faithful dog Shiro. He was a little white dog, not a pretty dog to look at, but he loved the farmer and his wife very much. And, since they had no children, they loved the dog like a little son. The happiest time of the day for the old farmer was the hour when he came home from the fields in the evening; then the dog Shiro would bark and lick his hand, and, while the old folks were eating their simple dinner, he would beg and get fed little pieces of the best food.

They were a very happy family, and troubled no one.

One day when the farmer came home Shiro did not run to meet him, but stood barking under a yenoki tree, digging the earth and barking. As the farmer came near, the dog ran to him, and pulled him by his clothes towards the tree. Then he started digging and yelping again.

The farmer couldn't imagine what the dog was after, but he took his spade anyway and helped Shiro to dig. After a while there was a clinking sound to the spade: but it was not a rock the farmer had struck — it was a gold coin! He dug farther, and found more. In half an hour he was rich! And Shiro, panting and happy, lay watching and wagging his silly tail.

Now this wonderful yenoki tree was near the fence that divided the farmer's land from his neighbour's, and a very mean neighbour this man Hato was. This Hato had watched the digging, and could hardly keep from hopping in his greed to get some gold for himself.

'Neighbour,' he said, 'lend me your little dog for a while, and maybe, with that wonderful nose of his, he can find *me* a golden tree!'

Of course the old farmer did not at all want to do this, because he knew Hato was mean to Shiro, and threw rocks at him if he so much as put his nose through the fence. But he was a kind man, and didn't know how to refuse. So next morning he let the neighbour take Shiro for the day, to hunt for gold.

That night, when the farmer came home, he missed his dog. He was too soft-hearted to go and ask his neighbour for him that night. But the next night the dog was still missing, so the farmer went to Hato, knocked politely on the door, and asked for Shiro.

You can imagine his sorrow when his neighbour told him roughly that the dog was dead!

This is what happened: Hato had taken Shiro out to his own yenoki trees. 'Dig, dig for gold,' he said, but Shiro just stood there with his tail between his legs, for he feared and hated the man. Then Hato had taken the dog by the neck, and forced his muzzle into the earth beneath each of the trees. At last, in desperation, the poor dog had begun to dig under one of them. Then Hato pushed him aside, and with his spade began to dig furiously. He hadn't dug for long when his spade struck against a covered jar in the earth, and he had got down on his knees and scraped away the dirt with his fingers in his eagerness.

He quickly scrambled to his feet, lifted the lid, and peered inside. There was a puff of smoke, a foul smell — and, heavy though it had seemed, the jar was empty.

In his anger Hato had picked up his spade and killed the poor dog with a terrible blow on the head. Then he threw the body into the hole he had dug, and tossed the earth back over it.

When the old farmer learned that his dog was dead, and had been buried under the yenoki tree, he asked if he might cut a branch from that tree to make a memorial for the faithful little animal.

Hato could not refuse, although he grumbled enough about it. When the farmer took home the branch, he and his wife decided that the best memorial they could make from it for poor Shiro would be a big new mixing spoon, for the old one was worn out, and a new one would remind them at every meal of the faithful pet who had always shared their simple food with them.

You can imagine their wonder when, every time they put a small handful of meal into the bowl with their new mixing spoon, more meal appeared, and more and more! It was magic, and they were sure that their faithful dog had a part in it, and was still watching over them although he was now only a spirit.

Neighbour Hato soon learned of the magical power of the old farmer's new spoon, and came over to borrow it. The farmer said no, and his wife said no; but Hato made such a bother about the matter, and said so many times that it came from his own tree, that at last they lent him the mixing spoon to get rid of him.

But two days, three days, passed, and Hato did not return it; so the farmer went to his door to ask for it.

'It's gone. I've burned it,' said Hato. 'Instead of always making more meal for me, it spoiled the meal I put with it. It turned the meal black, and made it smell. So I burned it. Look there – ' and he pointed to an end of the spoon still sticking out of his fire.

The poor farmer did not know what to do; but at last he asked if he might have the ashes of the mixing spoon to put in a jar as a remembrance of his dog Shiro. So he took home a jar of the ashes, and he and his wife decided to bury it under their yenoki tree. But as they were going down their garden, a puff of wind blew some of the ashes out of the jar.

It was early autumn, and all the trees had finished blooming; but wherever the ashes were blown against the branches, leaves and buds sprang to life. So the old couple knew that the ashes of the spoon were magic too. They were very quiet about the matter: but blossoms in October are noticed, and soon word got around that the farmer had some magic ashes that made trees bloom forever.

The tree came to life
(The Loving Dog)

Tortoise painted Leopard's coat
(*How the Leopard Got His Spots*)

All the cats, dogs, chickens . . . and people came out
(The Great Greedy Monster)

He called the magpies
(*The Star Princess*)

Soon a messenger came from the prince, summoning the old man and his ashes to the royal palace. There the farmer bowed low before his ruler, and told his story.

'My good man,' said the prince, 'in my garden there is a favourite cherry tree, which stands just outside my window, and which I love to look upon in its various seasons. I never tire of its blossoms in the spring, its greenery and fruit in summer, its bare twigs in the autumn, and its delicate snow-tracery in winter. But for the past year this tree has been dying, and I fear that this winter will be the end of it. Will you therefore try some of your magic ashes upon it, and see if you cannot bring it back to life?'

So the farmer went to the tree and uncovered his magic jar. No sooner had he sprinkled some of the ashes upon it, than the tree came to life again, and bloomed as though it were May. The prince was delighted, and sent the old farmer home loaded with money and with gifts.

Then Hato the evil neighbour thought that he would try the same trick. He had scooped up all the remaining ashes when he heard of the wonderful effects in his neighbour's garden; and now he went about the streets of the towns crying: 'Here is the man that can make trees bloom forever! Here is the man with the magic ashes!' The prince heard him calling in the streets, and sent for him.

'You are not the same man who put ashes on my tree,' said the prince.

'No, your lordship,' said Hato, 'I am not. But the man who came to you learned the secret from me, and stole some of my magic ashes.' So the prince put him to the test, asking him to make some of the bare trees in the garden bloom again.

Then Hato climbed into a tree, and shook out some of his ashes into the branches. At this moment an unlucky wind caught the ashes and blew them into the eyes of the prince, who howled with pain. And he roared with anger, too, when he could see again, for Hato's ashes had killed the trees they touched, and made them smell evilly.

Then Hato was put into prison for his mischief; and the old couple lived on contentedly without their bothersome neighbour; happy in the thought that their dog Shiro still was with them in spirit in the blooming tree of their garden.

Yes, all good dogs live on in Heaven!

The Star Princess

Traditional

Once upon a time in Japan there lived a farmer called
Mikeran, who spent every day working hard in the
paddy fields to make his living. One evening, feeling hot and
tired, he went down to the river to bathe.

He was just about to dive into the cool water when he
noticed a beautiful kimono, covered with feathers of many
colours, hanging on a tree by the river bank. He stretched
out his hand to touch it, but suddenly a cry came from the
river.

'Please, please don't take my kimono – I need it to fly back
to heaven.'

Mikeran turned to see in the water a beautiful woman
who shone like the stars.

'Oh, no,' he said, 'you must stay here, Star Princess. You
can come and live with me in the village and be my wife.'

The Star Princess cried and cried, and begged him to give
her back her kimono so that she could fly back to her home
in heaven, but Mikeran would not give in. And when he
reached home he hid the feather kimono beneath the bags of

rice and millet in his storeroom so that the Star Princess would never find it again.

Every day when her husband went out to work in the fields, the Star Princess would search for her kimono. She never found it until one day, when she was coming home from the village, she heard two children talking.

'I know a secret,' said the first child.

'What's that?' said the other.

'I know what Mikeran has hidden in his storeroom,' said the first.

'Well, tell me what it is,' said the other child impatiently.

'It's a feather kimono – and it comes from heaven!'

The Star Princess smiled to herself. She went straight to the storeroom and searched amongst the sacks of rice and millet until she found her kimono. But suddenly she realized how much she loved Mikeran and how lonely she would be without him. She decided that if she went back to heaven he must go with her. So she hid a message for him in the bellows by the fire and then, wrapping herself in the feather kimono, she flew up, up into the sky.

When Mikeran came home he found the house empty, and the storeroom door open. The feather robe has gone, he thought miserably, and my wife must have gone back to heaven.

He sat down by the fireplace and built himself a fire. But when he tried to blow up the fire with the bellows nothing happened. He looked inside the bellows and there was a piece of paper with a message written on it:

If you bury a thousand pairs of wooden clogs and a thousand pairs of straw sandals and then plant a bamboo tree above them, the bamboo will grow up to heaven itself.

Mikeran left home and set out to find a thousand pairs of sandals and a thousand pairs of clogs. But although he searched every corner of Japan he could only find nine hundred and ninety-nine pairs of sandals and nine hundred and ninety-nine pairs of clogs. However, he did as he had been told and buried the clogs and sandals. Then he planted a bamboo tree and sure enough it grew and grew until it reached far up beyond the clouds.

The Star Princess was sitting in heaven, weaving at her loom, when suddenly she heard a voice calling her. She looked down and saw a tiny figure clinging to the top of a tall bamboo tree, which stretched almost to heaven itself. She knew immediately it was her husband and reached down towards him with the shuttle of her loom. Mikeran caught hold of it and was lifted right into heaven itself.

The Star Princess was delighted to see her husband again, but her father, the king of all heaven, was not at all pleased – he did not want a poor and dirty farmer for a son-in-law. However, he knew it would take a clever plan to separate them again.

Finally, after much thought, the king of heaven had an idea. He invited his daughter and her husband to a magnificent feast and asked Mikeran if he would do him the honour of cutting the melons for the guests.

'This is how you must cut them,' he said. 'Take three melons together and slice them lengthways with your knife.' The Star Princess suddenly realized that her father was trying to trick Mikeran and leapt up with a cry, but it was too late. Mikeran sliced the melons and immediately a river sprang from them right across heaven, carrying Mikeran away on a tide of rushing water. And when the water finally subsided, the Star Princess and her husband found themselves on opposite shores of the river, with no bridge between them.

The king of heaven told them they must live apart forever, but the Star Princess cried and begged her father to let them be together, even if it could only be for one day a year. Eventually the king of heaven relented and on the seventh day of the seventh month he called all the magpies from all over the world, and they made a bridge across the river so that the Star Princess could cross over the river to her husband.

Every year, on the seventh day of the seventh month, July, the festival of Tanabata is celebrated all over Japan. People write what they most wish for on pieces of paper and pin them to bamboo trees, as they believe this is a lucky time when wishes will come true.

If you look up into the night sky you can still see Mikeran and the Star Princess — and the river that divides them. For the river has become the Milky Way, and Mikeran and the Star Princess the two stars, Vega and Altair.

How the Leopard Got his Spots

Traditional

A long time ago, the leopard had no spots, the zebra had no stripes, and the hyena was the most beautiful and proud animal in the jungle. But now these animals look very different, and this is how it happened.

One day Hyena was running through the jungle when he saw Tortoise gazing up at the fruit hanging from a tree above his head.

'Hyena,' cried Tortoise, 'please will you come and shake this tree with your strong paws, and bring down some of the fruit. I am so hungry, but the branches are too high for me to reach.'

Hyena laughed, baring his sharp white teeth. 'Of course I'll help you, Tortoise,' he said. 'I'll put you right up into the branches of the tree so that you can reach the fruit yourself.' Taking Tortoise between his strong jaws, he picked him up and put him on a branch high above the ground. Then off he ran, laughing at the poor, helpless tortoise.

Tortoise sat in the tree all day, afraid to move in case he fell. He was afraid to stretch out for any of the fruit. Hungry

87

and tired, he was still there by the time the sun had nearly set.

Then, swiftly and silently, Leopard bounded out of the twilight.

'Leopard! Leopard!' called Tortoise. 'Help! I'm stuck! I can't get down from this tree by myself.'

Leopard smiled kindly and immediately leapt up into the tree. He gently lifted Tortoise in his mouth and then jumped down again.

'Can I do anything else for you, Tortoise?' he asked.

'I'm very hungry,' said Tortoise. 'Could you shake the tree so that some of the fruit falls down?'

'Of course,' said Leopard, and he shook the tree until all the fruit had fallen to the ground. Tortoise would have plenty to eat for days and days.

Leopard was just about to run off into the darkness when Tortoise stopped him. 'I'd like to give you a present, Leopard,' he said, 'just to thank you. If you come back tomorrow when it's light, I will make you the most beautiful, the most magnificent animal in the whole jungle.'

The next morning Leopard returned and found Tortoise waiting for him with a box of paints and some paintbrushes. 'Leopard,' he said, 'I'm going to give you the most beautiful coat in the world. You will be the envy of every animal in the jungle.' And with his paints, Tortoise painted Leopard's coat with a rich and exotic pattern of dark spots.

When Tortoise had finished, Leopard walked away through the jungle. All the animals turned their heads and admired his beautiful new coat, and when Zebra saw him, he decided that he would go to Tortoise, too, and ask for a new coat.

'Please, Tortoise,' he said, 'will you paint my coat so that I look as beautiful as Leopard?'

Tortoise looked at him thoughtfully for a moment. Then he picked up his paints and painted Zebra's coat with stripes of black and white. When Tortoise had finished, Zebra galloped happily back into the jungle and all the animals congratulated him on his lovely new coat.

Now Hyena was very jealous when he saw how beautiful Leopard and Zebra looked, and he decided that he would go to Tortoise and pretend to be sorry for leaving him in the fruit tree. Then perhaps Tortoise would give him a lovely coat as well.

So off Hyena went to Tortoise, and said how sorry he was, and asked if Tortoise would paint his coat like Zebra and Leopard's.

Tortoise smiled.

'Certainly,' he said and picked up his paints. He painted for many hours, standing back from time to time to admire his work. When he had finished he sent Hyena off to show his new coat to all the other animals.

Hyena pranced proudly back into the jungle, his head held high. But all the animals just laughed and jeered at him. And when Hyena caught sight of his new coat in the river he knew why. Tortoise had painted his coat with a mess of dirty brown blotches. He was now the ugliest animal in the jungle.

Hyena slunk away into the furthest, darkest corner of the jungle to hide himself in shame. And to this very day hyenas only come out at night when no one can see their coats.

The Great Greedy Monster

Traditional

Once long ago in Africa there was a Great Greedy Monster. He was always hungry and would eat everyone and everything he could find. Whole villages and towns were swallowed up.

One day on his journey through the mountains he came to a narrow pass between two high walls of rock. As he put his enormous snuffling nose to the ground he smelt the smells of juicy cattle, goats, chickens – and people! And he knew that there must be a village on the other side of the mountains.

The Great Greedy Monster tried to get through the narrow pass between the rocks but he was too fat. For days and days he sat at its mouth, sniffing all the delicious smells from the other side of the mountain and growing hungrier and hungrier. In the end he grew so thin that he could just about squeeze his way through the pass.

There, in a valley hidden behind the mountains, the Great Greedy Monster found a village. He ate every chicken, every goat, every cow, every piece of fruit and every grain of corn in the village. And then he ate all the people as well.

But one woman escaped with her baby. For when she saw the Great Greedy Monster coming, she covered herself and her baby with cold ashes from the fire to hide their smell, and then hid in the corner of a hut. Although the Great Greedy Monster came sniffing round the door of the hut all he could smell was the rather unpleasant smell of ashes, so he went away again.

When the Great Greedy Monster had eaten everything in the village, he heaved and wobbled his fat body along the road back towards the mountains. But although he pushed and heaved, and pushed and heaved, he couldn't squeeze through the narrow pass between the rocks. He was stuck!

As the Great Greedy Monster couldn't move either forwards or backwards, he decided that he might as well just go to sleep. So he lay down, shut his eyes, and soon he began to snore.

Meanwhile, back in the village, the woman peeped out of the door of her hut to make sure that the Great Greedy Monster had gone. Then, leaving her baby on a pile of soft skins, she picked up a gourd and went down to the river to fetch some water to drink. When she came back, instead of her baby lying on the pile of skins, she found a great warrior, armed with a spear and shield, and many deadly knives. The woman was so surprised that she dropped the gourd and water ran all over the floor of the hut.

The warrior smiled. 'Don't be frightened, Mother,' he said. 'I am the same child you left behind when you went down to the river – the same baby you saved from the Great Greedy Monster. And now I'm going to take revenge on him.' And lifting up his spear and shield, the warrior set off towards the mouth of the pass, where the Great Greedy Monster's giant bottom could be seen bulging from the rocks.

The warrior crept quietly up behind the sleeping monster and leapt lightly onto his back. Then he plunged a spear into his neck. The Great Greedy Monster awoke with a roar, and struggled and thrashed his tail, but he was still stuck between the rocks and could not escape. As the warrior plunged the spear into his neck a second time, with a final howl, the Great Greedy Monster died.

Then suddenly, from inside the monster, there came a little voice:

'Let me out! Let me out!'

The warrior took his knife and cut into the Great Greedy Monster's body, and out of the monster's body came a little boy.

Then again from inside the monster came another sound:

'Woof woof! Woof woof!'

So the warrior cut further into the monster's side and out came a dog.

Then there came another sound from inside the monster:

'Cockadoodledoo! Cockadoodledoo!'

So the warrior cut further into the monster's side and out came a cockerel.

Then there came another sound from inside the monster:

'Moo-ooo! Moo-ooo!'

And the warrior cut further into the monster's side and out came a cow. Then the warrior cut and cut until he had cut a door in the side of the monster. And when he held it open all the cats, dogs, chickens, goats, cows and people from the village came out, and the nuts, corn, fruit and vegetables rolled out onto the ground.

All the people from the village were so happy that they made the warrior their chief and his mother their chieftainess. That night they had a great feast with music and dancing, and the sound of the drums could be heard right across the mountains. And the village lived in peace and happiness for many years.

Notes for Readers and Storytellers

The Hare and the Tortoise
Chratts – the crunching sound as the Hare eats his carrots.
Tsoukou, tsoukou – slowly, in her own good time (Greek).

The Fisherman and the Jinnee
Jinnee – also called *jinni, djinni, genie*. One of the class of spirits in Muslim mythology called the jinn. The jinn assume various sizes and shapes but often appear as huge and ugly men. They are composed mainly of fire.

The Enchanted Palace
Durbar – a king's court.
Shahnai – a woodwind instrument rather like a recorder and played at celebrations, particularly at weddings and coronations.
Chandan – a sandalwood perfume.
Fire – considered by the Hindus to be one symbol of God.
Five diamonds – five is considered to be an auspicious, or lucky, number by South Asians.

The publishers would like to thank the following for their kind permission to use copyright material in this anthology:

Luzac & Company and Jennie Ingham for *The Enchanted Palace* by Ashim Bhattacharya and Champaka Basu and *The Hare and the Tortoise* by Gabriel Douloubakas both © 1985 Jennie Ingham and first published in the Luzac Storytellers series; David Makhanlall for 'Brer Anansi and the Ghost' from *The Invincible Brer Anansi* © 1974 David Makhanlall and first published by Blackie and Son Ltd. Also for 'Brer Anansi and the Rainbow's End' from *The Best of Brer Anansi* © 1973 David Makhanlall and first published by Blackie and Son Ltd; the Peter Pauper Press for 'Ko-ai and her Lost Shoe' and 'The Willow-Leaf Eyebrow' from *Chinese Fairy Tales* by Sonia Roetter © 1946 and first published by the Peter Pauper Press. Also for 'The Loving Dog' from *Japanese Fairy Tales* by Lafcadio Hearn © Lafcadio Hearn 1948 and first published by the Peter Pauper Press.